Tackling Poverty

Catherine Chambers

Heinemann Library
Chicago, Illinois

www.heinemannraintree.com
Visit our website to find out
more information about
Heinemann-Raintree books.

To order:

☎ Phone 888-454-2279

▣ Visit www.heinemannraintree.com
to browse our catalog and order online.

Edited by Sarah Eason and Leon Gray
Designed by Calcium and Sarah Williams
Original illustrations © Capstone Global Library, LLC 2009
Illustrated by Geoff Ward
Picture research by Maria Joannou
Originated by Heinemann Library
Printed and bound in China by CTPS

13 12 11 10 09
10 9 8 7 6 5 4 3 2 1

Library of Congress Cataloging-in-Publication Data
Chambers, Catherine, 1954-
  Tackling poverty / Catherine Chambers.
    p. cm. -- (Headline issues)
  Includes bibliographical references and index.
  ISBN 978-1-4329-2410-2 (hc) -- ISBN 978-1-4329-2421-8
(pb)
  1. Poverty. 2. Poor. I. Title.
  HC79.P6C427 2008
  362.5--dc22
                          2008050152

Acknowledgments
The author and publishers are grateful to the following
for permission to reproduce copyright material:
Alamy Images: Bob Johns/Expresspictures.co.uk 5t,
Holger Leue/LOOK Die Bildagentur der Fotografen
GmbH 12, Les Stirling (Travel) 5b; Corbis: Lynsey
Addario 16, Pallava Bagla 9, Tim Brakemeier/EPA
26, Rick D'Elia 22, Andrew Holbrooke 15, Philippe
Lissac/Godong 21, Patrick Robert/Sygma 13, Law
Kian Yan/EPA 28; Istockphoto: Nicholas Fallows 17l,
Liza McCorkle 28–29, Paul Prescott 6; PA Photos/AP
Photo: Rebecca Blackwell 25, Saurabh Das 10–11, Diego
Giudice 18; Rex Features: Eye Ubiquitous 7, Sipa Press
24; Science Photo Library: Victor De Schwanberg 19;
Shutterstock: 4–5, 6, 7, 8–9, 10, 14–15, 17r, 18, 20, 22,
22–23, 27r, 29, Andrjuss 26–27, Ayakovlev.com 20–21,
Terry Chan 32, Pichugin Dmitry 16–17, Dhoxax 1, 8,
Kazi Mah-dee Hasan 3, 30–31, Nathan Holland 24–25,
Muriel Lasure 13bg, Inacio Pires 19, Salamanderman 10,
Kheng Guan Toh 12; Still Pictures: Joerg Boethling
11, 27.

Cover photograph reproduced with permission of
Corbis/Viviane Moos.

Every effort has been made to contact copyright holders
of material reproduced in this book. Any omissions will
be rectified in subsequent printings if notice is given to
the publisher.

Contents

Some words are printed in bold, **like this**. You can find out what they mean by looking in the glossary on page 30.

Poverty Scars the Planet

THERE IS POVERTY in every country in the world. The word *poverty* means different things to different people. However, all people who live in poverty share two things—they have no choice in life and very little opportunity to change their situation.

Poor in a rich land

Many countries are wealthy. These so-called **developed countries** include Australia, Japan, the United States, and some nations in Europe, such as Great Britain, France, and Germany.

Within these wealthy countries, there are still some people who live in poverty. These people are struggling to live their daily lives. They have few choices about the type of work they do. They have very little chance of improving their situation. They live in what is called "relative poverty."

Poverty and economy

Many countries are poor. These are called **developing countries** and include many nations in South Asia, large parts of South America, and parts of Africa south of the Sahara Desert.

Millions of people who live in the developing world cannot meet even basic needs of clean water, healthy food, a home, and access to health care and education. This type of poverty ranges from moderate to extreme poverty.

Tackling poverty

Many wealthy countries are trying to help the people who are living in poverty. They are trying to break the links in the poverty chain. In 2000 the **United Nations** (UN) pledged to end poverty by 2015, with 186 member states signing the agreement. Many people think this aim is unrealistic.

FACT!

✦ Around 1.5 billion people worldwide live in extreme poverty.
✦ Extreme poverty means living on less than one dollar a day.
✦ Every year, 8 million people die from the effects of extreme poverty.

MAKE POVERTY HISTORY

CLEAN UP TRADE RULES!

MAKE CHILD POVERTY HISTORY

Every year, thousands of demonstrations are held across the world to "Make Poverty History."

Many people in poor communities take whatever work they can. They earn only enough money to meet their basic needs.

Poor in the Country, Poor in the City

ILLIONS OF PEOPLE live in poverty in **rural** parts of Africa, Asia, and South America. Most farmers have only 1–2 hectares (2.5–5 acres) of land to farm. They rely on rainfall to water their **crops**. Farmers cannot produce enough food to feed their families and earn a living. Many flock to the cities to look for work.

Paved with poverty

In many **developing countries**, people who live in cities often have no job security. The work is tough and the pay is poor. Most live in crowded, unplanned towns called shantytowns or townships. They sleep in one-room houses made from cheap material, such as plastic.

Only a few earn enough money to send some back to their families.

Life on the farm

Farmers need to create more opportunities to continue living in rural areas, especially through trade. The farmers must grow food that can be sold in local markets or to other countries. Groups such as the Southern African Development Community help to increase trade between countries within their region. New crop varieties help to create wealth for the farmers, too. In KwaZulu-Natal, a low-cost cotton seed that is resistant to pests is producing more cotton.

Even in developed countries such as the United States, people live in poverty.

ON THE SPOT
Peru

Farmers in the CECOVASA **cooperative** in Peru no longer need to move to the big city of Arequipa to find work. Instead, they grow coffee plants near Lake Titicaca. In 1995 they became a Fairtrade cooperative. This means the farmers are given a fair price for the coffee beans they grow. There are more than 3,200 farmers in the cooperative. They export their coffee to the United States and Europe. CECOVASA is developing the community and other businesses.

Farmers in the CECOVASA cooperative are expanding into other areas of farming, such as cotton plants.

Education Paves the Way to Progress

THERE ARE ABOUT 875 million adults worldwide who cannot read or write. Many are poor people who have not had access to a teacher or a school. Without education, people become stuck in a cycle of poverty. Education helps them to become wealthier. Through reading skills they can find out how to grow more food, stay healthy, and develop business and communication skills.

Girls miss out

Education is taken for granted by many people. However, even today there are 121 million children in the world who cannot go to school. In the poorest countries, 46 percent of girls do not go to elementary school. Many stay at home to help out with the family or on the farm. They may have to walk miles every day to fetch water for the family.

Educating girls is important. Girls who go to school are more likely to find work and can pay for their own children to go to school. This helps break the cycle of poverty.

Airwave education

There are many ways to guide people into schools and colleges in **developing countries**. A new and exciting example is the Somali Distance Education Literacy Program. Since 2003, this program has used radio to educate adults in **rural** areas in East Africa. Students are taught by teachers over the radio. In the first year, 9,000 students passed exams in reading and writing, math, health care, the environment, and human rights.

A child learns how to play the guitar at a school for street children in Venezuela. Developing new skills helps to build confidence and break the poverty chain.

BEHIND THE HEADLINES

Computers are the key to a brighter future

Children from a rural village in India are shown how to use a laptop computer.

People use computers to access the Internet and improve basic skills in communication. In India, weatherproof computer kiosks have been set up in rural areas and poor parts of towns. They are easy to find near public buildings. Everyone in the community can use them.

Child Labor Leads to a Poor Future

Today, there are around 218 million child workers between the ages of 5 and 14. Some are as young as three. Most have to work to pay back family debt and medical bills.

Health and wealth

Most child workers live in South Asia. Millions more work in Africa and South America. In India, 70 percent of child workers are on farms. There they are often exposed to dangerous **pesticides**. Others work in small factories in cities for more than 10 hours every day. Many child workers make clothes for international clothing stores. The light is dim, and some child workers have bad eyesight. They often earn just 30 cents a day. Child labor is an easy way for the stores to make more money.

Tough action

Some groups publish guidelines about employing young people. **Convention** number 138 of the International Labor Organization points out that many jobs are unsuitable for children. However, **developing countries** often cannot afford to inspect all farms and factories. The job is often left to charities and volunteers, who report businesses that abuse the child workforce. The same charities set up schools and training programs to help young working people, too. In India, child workers have begun to protest for their own rights by joining organizations such as Free the Children.

A child works in a clothes factory in India. He works long hours but earns very little money.

ON THE SPOT
India

RUGMARK was set up by carpet makers and charities in India in 1994. This organization ensures that carpets or rugs made by any of its members did not involve child labor. It has set up schools to help children who were once made to work. Over four million RUGMARK rugs have been sold.

A RUGMARK logo shows that the product was made without child labor.

Good Health, Greater Wealth

POVERTY LEADS TO a poor diet and living conditions. This combination exposes people to disease. Adults who are sick cannot work. Their children often have to go to work instead and miss school. As adults, they will live in poverty, too. They may get sick and stop working. This vicious cycle is difficult to break.

Keeping people poor

Every year, millions of people die from **malaria**, **tuberculosis**, and **HIV/AIDS**. Millions more die from illnesses such as **pneumonia** and **diarrhea**. Often diseases are caused by poor housing, poor **sanitation**, and unclean water.

Another 2.2 million children die each year because they have not been **immunized** against dangerous diseases such as measles, tetanus, and tuberculosis. Children who are immunized grow up to be stronger adults.

Break the poverty cycle

Malaria is one of the world's biggest killers. Millions die every year. Mosquitoes spread the disease.

Insecticide-treated mosquito nets can save many lives in the developing world.

They breed in pools of **stagnant** water. Charities help local communities to clear up the pools. Insecticide-treated mosquito nets (ITNs) help to protect against mosquito bites at night. Between 2004 and 2006, the use of ITNs was increased in Kenya in East Africa. This reduced child deaths from malaria by 50 percent.

BEHIND THE HEADLINES

Paying the price for health care

Medical bills are often the most damaging expense to families in both the developing and the developed world. In India, many people lose their land to people who lend money to pay their medical bills. In the United States, 47 million people cannot afford health insurance. If they cannot afford the health care they need, they may not be well enough to work. This adds to the poverty cycle.

Free health clinics travel to remote parts of Africa to bring medical care to the people there.

Poorest Hit Hardest by Global Warming

A BLANKET OF gases, such as carbon dioxide and methane, trap heat around Earth. These gases exist naturally in the air, but many more are created by burning **fossil fuels**. This is causing **global warming**, which is making the planet warmer. **Developing countries** are suffering most from global warming. However, they are burning the least fossil fuels.

Dry desert, fierce flood

Around the world, **semideserts** and tropical grasslands are becoming much drier. Other parts of the world are being hit by extreme weather events such as **cyclones**. Some of the worst-affected areas are in parts of Asia, Africa, the Caribbean, and the United States. Many people in these areas already suffer from poverty.

As Earth's temperature rises, people in these areas will suffer more from illnesses such as **malaria** and **diarrhea**. The **World Health Organization** estimates that climate change has already led to 15,000 more deaths every year.

Fighting the effects

Developing countries are tackling climate change by sowing **crops** that resist drought. Other projects aim to reverse the effects of climate change. Countries in Africa are planting a Great Green Wall. This will be a 5-kilometer- (3.2-mile-) wide band of trees that stretches 7,000 kilometers (4,375 miles) across the continent. The trees will absorb harmful gases, hold soils together, and create new **ecosystems**.

Workers from Ethiopia plant tree saplings that will make new forests. By absorbing carbon dioxide, the trees will help to slow down global warming.

BEHIND THE HEADLINES
Bangladesh floods

The annual Bangladesh floods cover nearly 75 percent of the country. The government works with international aid agencies to prevent flood damage and provide relief. An organization called Islamic Relief is helping tens of thousands of people in the northeast by strengthening flood barriers and using early warning systems.

Many houses along the coast of Bangladesh are built on sticks. This protects them from the rising floodwaters.

Power Failure Hits the Poor

ABOUT TWO BILLION people worldwide do not have electricity or gas. Electricity is vital for lifting people out of poverty. Without it, everyday tasks take much longer, and there is no access to technology such as computers.

Natural energy

Countries are searching for **renewable energy** sources to replace **fossil fuels**. Many are now choosing **hydroelectric power (HEP)**, which uses energy from running water to generate electricity. Others are considering wind power in **rural** areas. It can power pumps to draw up water and **irrigate** fields.

Brazil and biofuels

Brazil is developing quickly. It has 600 HEP stations along many fast-flowing rivers. However, nearly half of Brazil's energy needs comes from **biofuels** made from sugarcane, ethanol gas, and **bagasse** (the waste from sugarcane fuel).

Sun power saves wood

Many poor people spend a lot of time looking for fuels such as wood to cook and keep warm. Firewood has become scarce, especially in the driest parts of the desert. In parts of rural Somalia, communities are using solar-powered stoves as well as wood and charcoal.

Solar-powered stoves have reduced wood burning by up to one-third in Somalia, in Africa.

ON THE SPOT
Sri Lanka

Many people in Sri Lanka spend up to 8 percent of their weekly income on power sources such as kerosene and dry-cell batteries. Things are becoming much better now that locally made **wind turbines** are generating electricity. The wind turbines can generate enough electricity to power batteries for lights and radios. Lights help to keep the elephants off valuable **crops**.

Elephants cause widespread damage to crops across Sri Lanka.

Bumpy Road to Poverty

POOR ROADS KEEP people in poverty. Farmers cannot get their **crops** to the market. Children cannot go to school. Companies will not invest in areas with poor roads. High fuel prices add to these problems.

Rough roads

In the developing world, many **rural** roads are not paved. They do not have a tarmac or concrete surface. Most are made from earth or hard **laterite** soils. Trucks and other heavy vehicles gouge deep tracks in roads, which fill with water when it rains. Heavy storms wash away the road surfaces.

Solving road problems

Vietnam has 210,000 kilometers (131,250 miles) of roads, but only 15 percent of them are suitable to drive on. People are tackling this problem by using local materials. They are using bamboo to make frames for road surfaces.

Danger on rough roads

Every year, more than 700,000 people die in road traffic accidents in the developing world.

Many are caused by roads that are badly designed and built. In poor city areas, millions live along narrow earth streets with no drainage. These streets can collapse in heavy rain. This is dangerous on steep slopes such as the **favelas** of Rio de Janeiro, Brazil. The streets there are being paved and concrete steps are being added.

Many accidents occur on the human-made roads that connect townships to cities.

Farmers should grow crops for biofuels:
Who is right and who is wrong?

FOR

The governments of many developed nations think that **biofuels** are the solution to using polluting **fossil fuels** such as coal and oil. Biofuels are a source of **renewable energy** and are much less expensive to produce than traditional fossil fuels.

Biofuels are made from crops such as corn. The corn is turned into ethanol, which can be used as a fuel.

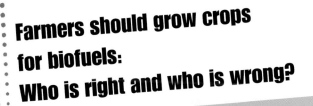

AGAINST

The world economy is crying out for biofuels, but this is forcing farmers from the developing world to grow these crops instead of traditional food crops. Farmers are growing so much biofuel that there is not enough room left to grow food for their own families.

Debt and Cash Flow Stop Development

People all over the world have to borrow money to pay for housing costs, medical bills, and even food. This debt can often plunge people into poverty. In the developing world, some people give up some of their land to pay back the debt. Others use their food **crops** to pay or let their children work for no pay.

Community banks

Tackling debt is hard because people who lend the money charge **interest** to the people who borrow. So, the borrowers pay back more money than they borrowed. A solution is the local community bank. This bank does not charge heavy interest rates.

Mobile cash flow

Getting cash when people need it is often a problem in the developing world. Sometimes people wait for months for money, loans, or grants from banks or family members. One solution works well in Kenya. This is the "M-Pesa" program set up by a communications company called Safaricom.

The "M-Pesa" program allows people to send money to people or make a donation by sending a text message on a cell phone. The money is collected by a local registered agent and distributed to where it is needed. Many city workers send money back to their families this way. Even small donations can help to fight poverty by getting cash to people quickly.

In Kenya, Safaricom registered more than 20,000 new customers within a month of opening in March 2007.

Register FREE at any Authorised M-PESA Agent

M-PESA Send pesa by phone
M-PESA is the new, easy and affordable way to send money home.

MAGNATE TEL: 550950-4

ON THE SPOT
Bangladesh

Many women in Bangladesh now run their own small business.

For more than 30 years, women in Bangladesh have benefited from small business loans called **microcredit** agreements. Now, women are forging ahead through the Bangladesh Women Chamber of Commerce and Industry. This helps women develop their skills, learn new technologies, and have a voice in business.

◆ The oldest type of community bank is the credit union, which began more than 150 years ago.
◆ Microcredit agreements have helped millions of people raise their standard of living.
◆ In 2007 Kenya opened its first Islamic bank, the First Community Bank (FCB) Ltd.

FACT!

Prejudice Fuels Poverty

SOME PEOPLE ARE left in poverty because of their **class**, color, religion, or **gender**. They are often given the worst jobs or no jobs at all. They live in poor housing and may suffer abuse by people in positions of authority. Most countries have laws that stop this prejudice, but it still goes on.

People against prejudice

Tackling prejudice starts by finding out about the skills and potential of people from every walk of life.

Most of South Africa's black community still lives in the poorest housing. White people usually live in the best homes.

Women often struggle against poverty and prejudice the most. In **developing countries**, banks and companies have found that lending money to women is usually a good business decision. Women often use money to develop their own small businesses. They pay back the loan quickly and educate their children with their profits. This is helping to break the poverty cycle.

Traveling communities

Europe's community of traveling people is one of the poorest in the world. Travelers suffer from a lot of prejudice, and they receive little support. In Hungary, between 60 and 70 percent of travelers are unemployed. In Britain, 20 percent live in absolute poverty.

There are ways to educate people on the move. Somalian children of traveling farmers go to schools run by the Pastoral and Environmental Network in the Horn of Africa. They teach environmental skills and animal care, as well as reading, writing, and math skills.

It is still impossible for people born into the Dalit group to move out of this social class.

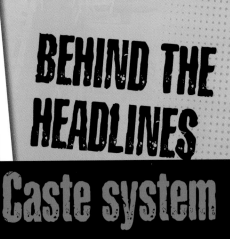

BEHIND THE HEADLINES
Caste system

The **caste** system on the Indian subcontinent groups people into social classes that always stay wealthy or poor. The caste system is outlawed in India, but many people still follow it. The **Dalit** community is one of the lowest social classes. They are below even the poorest caste. So, most Dalits get the worst and dirtiest jobs and the poorest housing. There are 160 million Dalits who live in India. The government is trying to set up free education for them to help them out of poverty.

War Brings Greater Poverty

WAR BRINGS POVERTY to people in every part of the world. It takes away young people who could help to build their communities. It makes people afraid to go out into the fields to grow their **crops**. Many people become **refugees**. They have to leave their homes and live in other countries.

War makes poverty

The Office of the **United Nations** High Commissioner for Refugees (UNHCR) helps refugees. It also helps people who are displaced within their own country. The agency understands that refugees often arrive in countries that are already poor.

Almost half of the refugees helped by UNHCR are from the wars in Iraq and Afghanistan. Many Iraqis have fled to nearby Syria and Jordan. The UNHCR supports food aid, health care, and education for the refugees there.

Peace can lift poverty

Local and international projects can help to put communities back together after war. Each situation has different needs. After conflict in Sri Lanka, roads needed to be rebuilt. Irrigation systems were mended and farmers' organizations were set up again. These measures helped farmers grow rice again, so the country had food once more.

Following the Iraq War that started in 2003, many Iraqis fled to neighboring Syria to live as refugees.

ON THE SPOT
Sierra Leone

Between 1991 and 2002, a terrible civil war waged inside Sierra Leone in West Africa. One million people had to leave their homes for fear of being killed. Houses were destroyed and essential services were put out of action. When the war in Sierra Leone ended in 2002, a spice-growing project was set up to bring farmers back to their land. One project involved sowing ginger seed sent from China. By 2006 Sierra Leone was exporting ginger. Tourism is also slowly developing along the country's miles of beautiful golden beaches.

Many young men suffered serious injuries as soldiers in Sierra Leone, but they are rebuilding their lives now that the war is over.

✦ The UN estimates that more than 250,000 child soldiers are involved in wars around the world.
✦ Myanmar, in Southeast Asia, has one of the highest numbers of child soldiers serving in its state army.

FACT!

Going Global— Good or Bad?

IN 1981 THE world's most powerful leaders agreed to tackle poverty through globalization. This means letting countries and companies sell goods wherever they want to and putting money into businesses anywhere in the world.

Good for the rich

Globalization has not worked for most **developing countries**. Only Southeast Asia has seen a difference over the last 25 years. Some **developed countries** have used globalization to control trade in the developing world. They have used it to get the prices they want for **crops** such as coffee and rice.

The world's eight most powerful countries, called the G8, set up many trade rules. They are allowing five developing countries to join their meetings. This new group of countries will be called the "G8 plus 5."

Small is beautiful

Small farms and businesses in developing countries cannot compete with those in the West, so many join forces as **cooperatives**. As a group, they install electricity, running water, and **sanitation**. They buy new technologies, such as computers and machinery, to build their businesses.

The leaders of the world's most powerful countries meet during a summit in Japan in 2008.

ON THE SPOT
Kenya

The Finlay Flower Farm near Kericho in Kenya's Rift Valley sells cut flowers around the world. The farm belongs to the Fairtrade Foundation, which ensures that growers get good prices for their products. The workers at the farm learn computer skills and attend other training courses. The company has also set up housing projects, clinics, and schools.

Kenya

Rift Valley

Kericho

Indian Ocean

A worker harvests Fairtrade roses at a flower farm in Kenya, in East Africa.

Get Involved!

Sometimes people face sudden poverty, and the world has to help quickly. This is especially true during natural disasters, such as the 2006 **tsunami** that devastated Asia and parts of East Africa. However, governments, international organizations, and aid agencies concentrate mostly on trying to end long-term poverty.

It is hard to strike the right balance between saving people's lives in a disaster and building for the future. It stretches the world's resources, organizational skills, and imagination.

Promise to end poverty

Every year, the world's wealthiest countries promise billions of dollars in aid. Despite this, some never pay up.

In April 2008 the G8 nations agreed to double aid to **developing countries** by 2010. This means that over $80 billion will be available to fund new projects. These include training six million teachers for schools. The European Union (EU) has made each country promise to pay what they said they would pay. We can only wait to see if they keep their promises.

Workers load up aid trucks for the victims of the 2008 Myanmar flood. The government in Myanmar did not take in aid for a long time because it does not trust the West.

THINGS TO DO

Start small

- Small steps lead to giant strides. Some of the most successful projects start small. They work because they involve the people they are helping. People in poverty know how to make their lives much better—they just need help to achieve their goals.

Get political

- Use your knowledge to write to local politicians. What are they doing to help stop the cycle of poverty? Is the government using aid funds properly?

Fairtrade shopper

- Choose what you buy carefully. Buy Fairtrade products whenever you can. Look for the Fairtrade logo to be sure a product is Fairtrade.

Seek out sponsorship

- See if your school, community group, club, or family would like to sponsor an anti-poverty project in another country.

A sponsored cow will provide children with healthy milk. It will also bring milk products that the family can sell for cash.

Help raise money

- You could try to set up a money-raising event on June 12 every year. This is "World Day Against Child Labor."

Glossary

bagasse waste product from sugarcane biofuel. Bagasse is reused as a fuel.

biofuel fuel made from plant parts such as palm oil seeds and sugarcane

caste economic and cultural group into which many people are born in the Indian subcontinent

class group of people who share a similar background and way of life

convention agreed set of standards

cooperative group of people who share resources to build up a business

crop plant grown by farmers

cyclone rotating storm with fierce winds and heavy rain

Dalit large group of people who are treated as the lowest social class in the Indian subcontinent

developed country rich country

developing country poor country

diarrhea stomach infection that leads to a dangerous loss of fluid

ecosystem system of climate, plant, and animal life

favela poor township in Brazil

fossil fuel fuel such as oil, coal, and gas. These fuels formed from the remains of plants and animals.

gender male or female

global warming increase in the average temperature at Earth's surface

HIV/AIDS viral infection that breaks down the body's immune system

hydroelectric power (HEP) electricity that is generated by the force of running water

immunize protect against disease

interest extra money that has to be paid back when money is borrowed

irrigate take water from rivers and lakes through a system of pipes and channels to water the land

laterite hard type of soil

malaria infectious disease caused by germs that spread through the bites of some types of mosquitoes

microcredit small loan to set up a business or pay for training

pesticide chemical sprayed on crops to kill insect pests

pneumonia disease caused by a germ that usually causes an inflammation of the lungs

refugee person forced to leave his or her home or country because of a crisis

renewable energy fuel from natural materials that can be easily grown again

rural relating to the countryside

sanitation drainage systems for dealing with sewage and the water used for washing

semidesert area neighboring a desert and another type of land

stagnant allowed to stand still for a long time

tsunami series of giant waves caused by earthquakes on the ocean floor

tuberculosis disease caused by a germ that usually attacks the lungs

United Nations international organization to preserve peace

wind turbine machine turned by wind to make electricity

World Health Organization public health agency of the United Nations

Find Out More

Books

Green, Robert. *Poverty (Global Perspectives)*. Ann Arbor: Cherry Lake, 2008.

Mason, Paul. *Poverty (Planet Under Pressure)*. Chicago: Heinemann Library, 2006.

Senker, Cath. *Poverty (What If We Do Nothing?)*. Milwaukee: World Almanac Library, 2007.

Simons, Rae. *AIDS and Poverty (All About AIDS)*. Nunda, N.Y.: AlphaHouse, 2008.

Websites

Unicef is the largest global organization working especially for children. Find out what this important organization is doing to help children break the cycle of poverty:
www.unicef.org

Learn more about how poverty affects children in the United States at this website of the National Center for Children in Poverty:
www.nccp.org

This UN-sponsored website aims to educate, inspire, and empower young people to fight against global poverty:
www.netaid.org

This website is run by the charity DATA, which aims to end extreme poverty and HIV/AIDS in Africa. The rock star Bono is one of the organization's cofounders:
www.data.org

Index